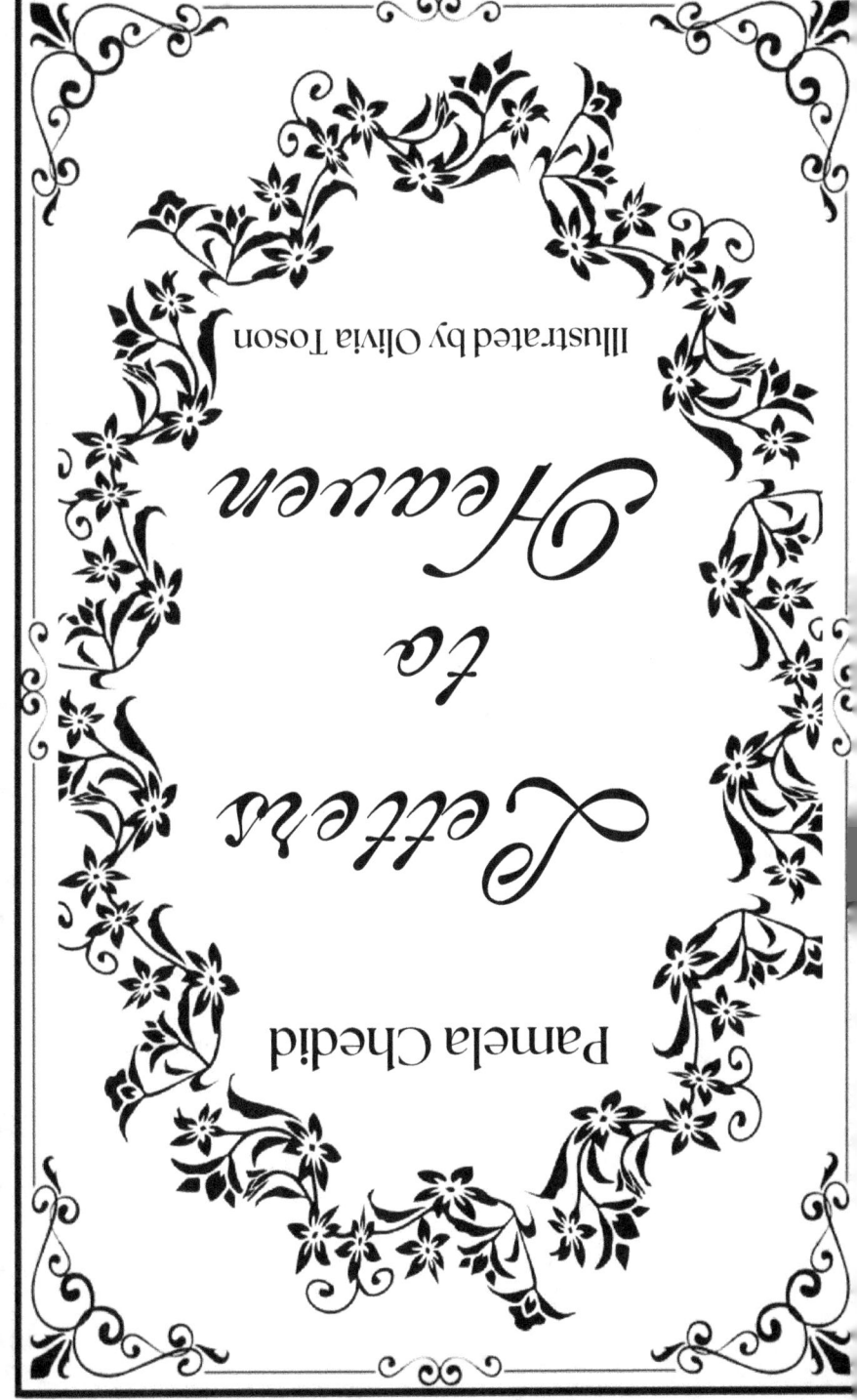

Letters to Heaven © Copyright 2025 Pamela Chedid

Illustrated by Olivia Toson

All rights reserved. Except for quotations, no part of this book may be reproduced or transmitted in any form or by any means, electronic or mechanical, including photocopying, recording, uploading to the inter-net, or by any information storage and retrieval system, without written permission from the publisher.

www.parousiamedia.com | ISBN: 978-1-923430-44-0

For Jesus,

my perpetual lighthouse

Jesus is *my* poet,

nothing speaks to me like His word

Contents

Part 1

I wished	13
The Beginning and the End	14
Mother of Mercy	16
The wood of my Lord's cross	17
Who do you say I am?	18
On you my Lord	20
My Lord who rescues	23
Jesus who is everything	24
Back to Calvary	26
Jesus Mercy	30
Mary Mother of God	33
Thank you Lord	34
Never Truly Gone	35
Eucharist to Adore	37
The space between you and me	39
A walk with Jesus	41
The day I fell	42
His Holy Plan	46
His Divine Mercy	47
Holy Spirit	49
What did I see?	50
His Holy Feet	51

Part 2

Jesus our King is born	56
Palm Sunday Glory	57
That Day	58
Risen!	60
Holy Communion Gift	61
Child of God	62
Love without Christ	63
Angel of Mine	65
Jesus my Friend	66

Part 3

Saint Michael	73
Saint Anthony	74
Saint Rita	76
Saint Padre Pio	77
Saint Joseph	79
Saint Francis of Assisi	80
Saint Maximilian Kolbe	81
Saint Bernadette	83
Saint Charbel	85

Part 1

Wished

I wished to be a splinter of wood
On the day you died on the cross my Lord
To be a speck of dust that settled on your skin
Or a drop of the vinegar from which you drank
To be a fibre of the cloth that draped your body
Or a thorn that crowned your head
To be the wind that carried your breath
Together with the sun that reflected your glory
To be the good thief and be forgiven
But most of all, I wished to be me
Present at the foot of your cross
To be washed by your holy side when your
precious blood spilled down towards the earth

John 19:28-37

13

The beginning and the end

It was early morning and I could not sleep
Endless voices of things to feel and weep
I took my load and gave it rest
And found my bible on my chest
So many worries, so much fear
I needed to feel my Lord near
So I began to read and Revelations took hold
Of things I'd heard, seen and been told
I'd read this book many times before
But this time was different
This time when reading I knew for sure
We did not listen, turned away from prayer
We failed to hear you
Let's be fair
You asked us to leave it all and follow you
But we were deaf and chose the lonely road
Of greed, gluttony and the selfie mode

Now this plague is here and it lies in your hands
And spreading rapidly across all your lands
You had no choice but to make us stop,
To slow down and take a look
Just as it was written in your book
Now the end is close, it's etched in stone
For all, not just me alone
"I am the Alpha and the Omega, the first and the last,
the beginning and the end
It was because of you I chose my son to send"
So let's take hands, rosaries and prayer
Let's use this time to love and share
Remember to take His Word and read
As He has sowed the blessed seed
"I am coming soon"
I am waiting for you, Jesus
Together with your blessed Mother, dressed with the
sun and the moon

Revelation 12:1-3
Revelation 22: 7-17

Mother of Mercy

Mother of Mercy oh Mother of Light
I heard you call my name last night
I took some time to be still and made no sound
Perhaps in me a voice you found
You've told us many times before
Down on your knees! You seemed to implore
Our ears were deaf,
We could not hear... we failed to see the dangers near
I wondered how could we make this right?
For God was angry, he cried out with might
Return to your homes and remember me
I am the way, the light don't you see?
Mother of God, in fear we stand
Our homes are made on pillars of sand
What should we do, can you calm him down?
You give me a look, perhaps even a frown
My son is sad, he's full of sorrow
But perhaps things will be better tomorrow
Remember to pray, he taught you the way
And still you ask me, you don't know what to say?
Take hold of your beads, and remember His Glory
Reflect on His life: it's the most beautiful story
And take a moment to sit and be at His will
Feel Him in your heart, He lives there still!

The wood of my Lord's cross

The wood of my Lord's cross covers me and protects me from attacks of the foe

The wood of my Lord's cross upholds me and repels me from dangers below

The wood of my Lord's cross sanctifies me and cleanses my heart and soul

The wood of my Lord's cross embraces me and graciously makes me whole

The wood of my Lord's cross promises me and frees me from the stain of sin

The wood of my Lord's cross guides me so all spiritual battles I win

The wood of my Lord's cross rejoices with me for its lumbers are bound with love

The wood of my Lord's cross is a gift for me, sent from the Father above

The wood of my Lord's cross leads me to the place of the heavenly sea

The wood of my Lord's cross ultimately sets me free

Luke 23:26

Who do you say I am?

I say you are Jesus the true King

Who do you say I am?

I say you are goodness since only love you bring

Who do you say I am?

I say you are the voice of reason, my soul you sustain

Who do you say I am?

I say you are the healer who takes away my pain

Who do you say I am?

I say you are the Son of Man

Who do you say I am?

I say you are my strength which tells me I can

Who do you say I am?

I say you are Jesus my friend

Who do you say I am?

I say you are the Christ I defend

Who do you say I am?

I say you are my conscience and heart

Who do you say I am?

I say you are my shadow for we are never apart

Who do you say I am?

I say you are my refuge and home

Who do you say I am?

I say you are my company when I am alone

Who do you say I am?

I say you are the strength in my grief

Who do you say I am?

I say you are my greatest relief

Who do you say I am?

I say you are the pathway to heaven

Who do you say I am?

I say without you I am lifeless and barren

Matthew 16: 13-19

On you my Lord

Set my gaze upon you oh Lord
And let me not sway left or right
Hold me steadfast upon your cross
Throughout the temptations of the night
Set my gaze upon you oh Lord
For the road is wide and deep
Help me to avoid all sin
It's my soul I wish you keep
Set my gaze upon you oh Lord
And cut me off from the earth
For nothing that comes from this world
Has any abiding sense of worth
Set my gaze upon you oh Lord
And unite me with your love

Send your Holy Spirit to guide me
And protect me with your sacred dove
Set my gaze upon you oh Lord
So that when I fall I kneel
And lay it out before you Lord
It's my soul I wish you heal
Set my gaze upon you oh Lord
And shower me with your grace and wisdom
So on that day when you bid me come
I'm made worthy of entering your kingdom

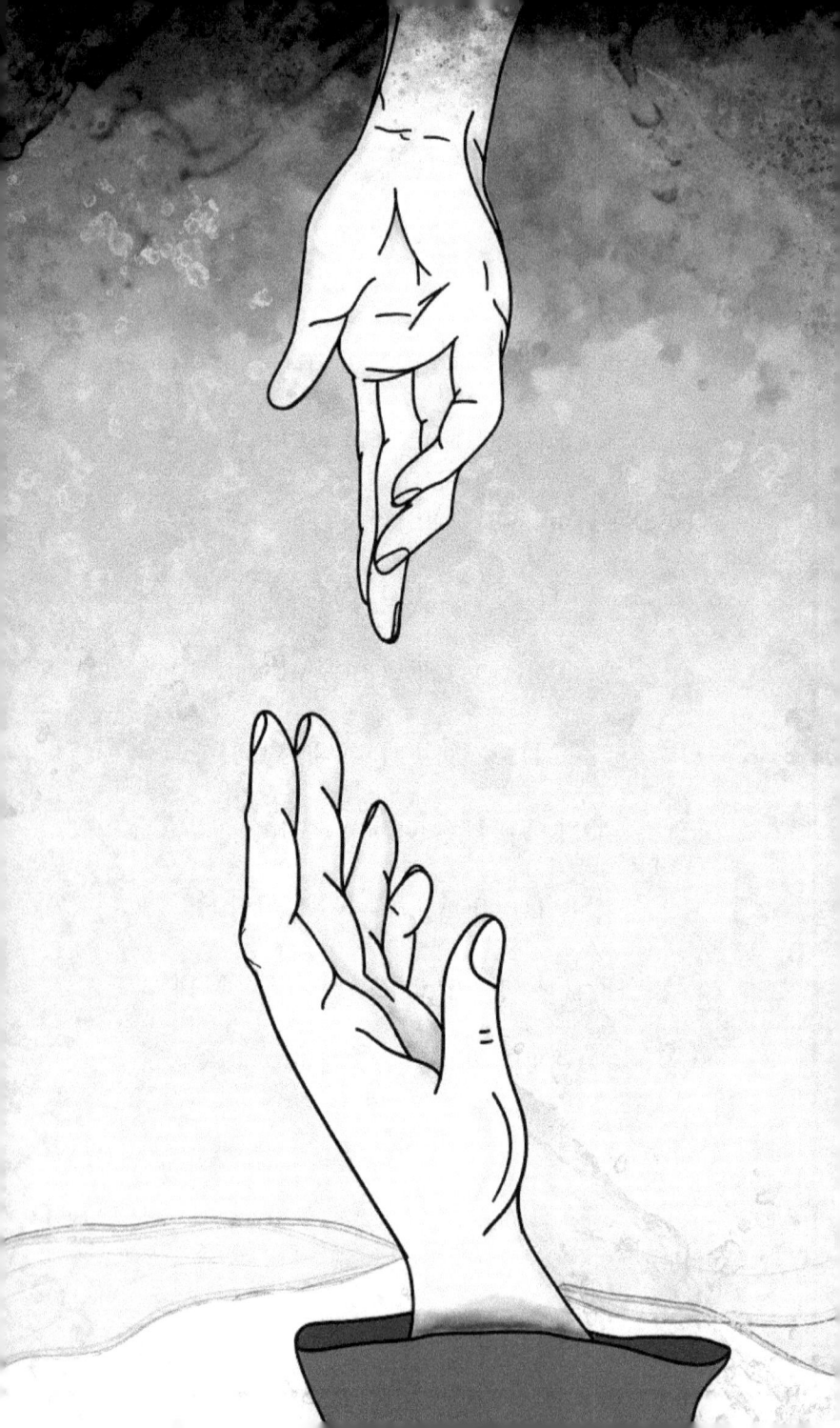

My Lord who rescued

Dear Lord
I come to you today
To take this pain away
For someone whom I love has gone another way
I saw them adrift in a dark coloured boat
Along a windy coast, no paddle or sail keeping them afloat
So walk across the ocean and take them by the hand
Lead them to the shore and back onto dry land
For this task is too great for me
I can't swim, you see
So if it be your will
You'll take them in your palm
Fill them with your goodness and a longing sense of calm
Remind them of your enduring love
And that you're always watching from above
And let that windy coast be no more
Just a tiny little whereabouts, visible safely from the shore

Matthew 8:23-26

23

Jesus who is everything

Jesus you are everything

Most almighty Lord,

the one who looks for you will always find love

Jesus, who forgives, provide absolution to the sorrowful

Jesus, ever calming, console the anxious

Jesus, our friend, comfort the lonely

Jesus, the righteous, free those who are afflicted

Jesus, the light of the world, deliver us
from plagues and disease

Jesus, the creator, protect the unborn child

Jesus, the teacher, give direction to the misguided

Jesus, the saviour, deliver us from our earthly worries

Jesus, King of hearts, draw us nearer to you

Jesus, King of peace, restore peace to our hearts and homes

Jesus, the Shepherd, gather those who wonder astray

Jesus, Light of the world, help those who suffer in darkness

Jesus, the One True Voice, speak for those who are silenced

Jesus, the Protector, deliver us from the evil one

Jesus, Son of God, bring peace to those who mourn

Jesus, the Holy Doctor, heal our bodies and minds

Jesus, the Holy Child, bring us final rest in your eternal home

Back To Calvary

I saw my Lord Jesus dressed like a king
But his face was wounded and what sorrow did it bring
I knew not what to do
For he seemed so upset
My heart ached with confusion and terrible regret
Where to begin?
Could I bandage each sore?
The wounds were countless
Into his flesh they tore
I looked into his eyes
Two ponds made of sorrow
But they managed to flicker up
And the angels did follow,
He turned on the road with the wood on his back
Slowly dragging the cross up the paved rocky track
Confused in my heart I asked him with dread,
"Lord, where are you going?"

Then he turned to me softly lowering his head,
"Back to be crucified."
Those words cut my soul and I understood it to be
My sins were the reason he was carrying that tree
So I asked him once more,
"How many times have you done that for me?"
I ran to his feet and dropped in surrender,
And heard his voice perfectly answer,
"My child, your sins are forgiven, I choose not to remember".

Hebrews 8:12

Jesus Mercy

Jesus mercy, I beg you forgive

My sins of today

And those of tomorrow

The sins that I committed and caused you much sorrow

Those of my youth and those of old age

Those that caused our relationship to change

Forgive the ones I wish I could forget

Especially those which cause me much regret

The ones with knowledge and those without

The ones where my faith was replaced with doubt

The ones I committed but went back for more

All the times you were silent, and wouldn't keep score

The ones that have been and those still to come
The ones from my flesh and those from my tongue
The ones that afflict you and all those that offend
And the ones that deserved me a terrible end
Lord Jesus I beg you forgive
Grant me your pardon
And allow me to join you in your kingdom
Where forever you live

Psalms 51:1-10

Mary Mother of God

Mother of Christ conceived without sin
Chosen by God to be sanctified even as you begin
Mirror of justice and tower of love
Your radiant beauty comes from heaven above
Oh compassionate and merciful mother
Your love for your children is like no other
Cover us with your holy mantle
And be our perpetual protection in every battle
Intercede for us before your son
For you are our hope, Holy Immaculate one
Holy Mother of God purest in heart
Bring us to Jesus so we are never apart,
Deliver our prayers to your son's holy ear
We trust with your help we have nothing to fear
Most Blessed Mother of God, remain with us still
So that we may forever thank you and never abandon His
Holy Will!

Luke 1:26-38

33

Thank you Lord

Dear Lord
Thank you for the sun and moon in the sky
And the stars that appear up high
Thank you for my children and the love of my days
Who fill me up in so many different ways
Thank you for my family and friends
And the love and memories that transcend
Thank you for the tears in my eyes
It's a picture of your sorrows and sighs
Thank you for my life and my being
And the beauty of eternal living that you're guaranteeing
Thank you for the world and the wonders that you send
And the worries that you always amend
Thank you for the suffering and sadness that I feel
And the mysteries you chose to reveal
Thank you for coming to show me the way
And the promise to take me to heaven one day

Never Truly Gone

To the living, I am no more

To the mourning, I am at peace

To the crying, I am smiling

To the wondering, I am listening

To the praying, I am interceding

To the lost, I am found

To the aching, I am comforted

To the weak, I am strong

To the sick, I am restored

To the heartbroken, I am loving

To the searching, I am waiting

Dream of me and I will visit you

Speak to me and I shall hear you

Pray to me and I shall comfort you

Remember me and I shall be with you and

never truly gone

Eucharist to Adore

Love of Jesus in the Eucharist, forgive me

Hidden Jesus in the Eucharist, seek me

Spiritual nourishment of Jesus in the Eucharist, feed me

Peace of Jesus in the Eucharist, console me

Wonder of Jesus in the Eucharist, amaze me

Word of Jesus in the Eucharist, speak to me

Courage of Jesus in the Eucharist, carry me

Mystery of Jesus in the Eucharist, reveal yourself to me

Humility of Jesus in the Eucharist, humble me

Blood of Jesus in the Eucharist, cleanse me

Body of Jesus in the Eucharist, heal me

Heart of Jesus in the Eucharist, deliver me

Voice of Jesus in the Eucharist, call me

Living God, Jesus in the Eucharist, save me

Mark 14:22-24

Luke 22:14-20

The space between you and me

I often think about the space between you and me
Where are you my Lord?
Hidden in a place that I can't see
I dream about your face
I sit still, blind
Tracing your features with my hands
Imagining your face together piece by piece
And what of your voice?
I strain to hear you
The silence is deafening
Why are you so far away my Lord?
I ache to hear you, to see you and feel you near
Then the space between us becomes very small
And we are bound
Can the scent of a rose be separated from its petals?
Or sand be parted from the ocean?
Nor can daylight be divided from the sun
Holy Spirit you fill me
And the space between you and me
Becomes nothing but love

Psalms 13:1-6

A walk with Jesus

I'd like to take a walk with you
And wade across a knee high plain
To answer all my questions and listen as you explain
I'd like to feel your hand and have it heal my soul
To spend precious time with you as we take a little stroll
I'd ask you about the past and how it came to be
And what of the future, all you've planned for me
I'd love to pick some flowers and ask you how they're made
And how you placed the scent inside
and watch the colours fade
I'd like to say I'm sorry and how much I felt I've lost
Each every time I broke your heart
and denied you on the cross
Then you'd turn to me and kiss my head
and say you don't keep score
That because of you my failures aren't counted any more
You assure me that I'm enough and that's all you have to say
We press on together in silence, perfect in every way

The day I fell

The fog was thick and obscuring
As I headed on my way
A not too distant journey I'd set aside to pay
The day seemed just the same
The road I'd done before
A familiarity that spoke to me in a
voice I could recall
Little lights lit up the path
With tiny rays of righteousness
But caught unaware I tripped
and fell fooled by darkness
Perhaps it was the fog or perhaps it was my pride
Above all my gaze had fallen from the cross
and off towards the side

I felt a pang of anguish, my heart was ripped apart
The fall had turned me away from
His Holy Sacred Heart
I dared not look up for I'd lost my state of grace
But moved inside I closed my eyes and his wounds
I found my hands embrace
Singing a song of sorrow
Through the priest I did confess, and instantly I felt
myself cured from the depths of my distress
And so I continued along that path
the Lord had planned for me
No fog - just sunshine
For the Lord had forgiven me

John 20:23

His Holy Plan

There was a small journey you'd planned for me
Alone in darkness, I sailed the sea
The nights were cold and the days were long
A boundless horizon, where did I belong?
You knew my heart and the tears it shed
The blood of my soul was full of dread
But you were there, I just couldn't see
A time for bonding, just you and me
This time was ours and you meant it so
You wanted my faith in you to grow
So hold my hand and lead the way
Heal my sickness and worries today
And whichever way the wind may blow
Remind me, with my struggles, your love grows
And if it be your will, let this cup pass by me
My future you determine and that sets me free

Psalms 119:145-160

46

His Divine Mercy

Over the hills where the sun meets the sky
He met a young man with a tear in his eye
His clothes were heavy like the weight of a stone
As he stood in the field lost and alone
He'd taken the wrong road and was out of his way
Away from his loved ones he seemed to stray
The load was too heavy to turn back now
It seemed impossible, he didn't know how
"Unload on me," he heard Him say
"My mercy is great, I'll show you the way!"
The man looked up from the depths of despair
What he'd heard didn't seem fair
He wanted to hide under the mountain of shame
Forget who he was, resign from his name
But the Lord smiled and outstretched his hand
"My mercy is infinite, no sin is too great
Trust in my mercy, there's no need to wait!"

Holy Spirit

Holy Spirit oh eternal flame
Holy Heaven cries out your blessed name
Come into my heart and make me whole
You hold the key to saving my soul
Be my blanket and protect me from the cold
Cover me with your light as I grow old
Become my refuge and give me rest
Help me lean on you and your holy breast
Wipe my tears when I cannot see
Help me to trust in you and let things be
Stir a wind in me like a raging storm
Cleanse me like a new dawn
Give me the words you want me to say
Be my light and guide the way
Quench my thirst in your holy rivers
Become my calmness when my heart quivers
Oh Holy Spirit, oh luminous dove
One with the Spirit, one with your love
When the day shall come that I kneel by your throne
Promise to find me a place in your home

John 14:15
Acts 2:1-4

What did I see?

I looked upon His cross and what love did I see?
The goodness of the world had sacrificed himself for me
I looked upon His cross
And what tenderness did I see?
His silence which spoke to me and danced inside of me
I looked upon His cross and what beauty did I see?
His arms outstretched upon that tree
as he embraced the world and me
I looked upon His cross and what sadness did I see?
The tears of Heaven raining down on Him
and falling from that tree
I looked upon His cross and what passion did I see?
The love burning out of Him and spilling over me
I looked upon His cross and what joy did I see?
The Holy Face of Jesus was smiling down at me

His Holy Feet

My Lord granted me a look at his feet,
A flashing of light or vision so sweet
I saw them crossed over at the foot of his cross
A reminder of the day when so much was lost
I wanted to be near them and caress them so
To kiss them and hold them and not let go
It was but a second at most or two,
But still I wondered, what did he want me to do?
It took me some time to understand and see
That dream was a gift from him to me
In silence I knelt searching for grace
There in that moment I found my place
He called me to linger, to persevere, to learn,
To embrace his teachings and wait for my turn
To walk in his footsteps towards his light,
To share in his love and to do what's right
So now I endeavor to live as he'd wish
To serve with compassion, to love and to cherish
Each day is a gift and a chance to grow near
To find strength in his presence and cast off all fear
With his feet as my compass my heart will abide
The grace of his love forever my guide

Part 2

Jesus our King is born

Angels sung high and stars shone bright

On the very first Christmas night

It was a manger they found to give him rest

Marked by a star, glowing bright in the east

Joseph and Mary knelt down to pray

Adoring baby Jesus asleep on the hay

Three wise men heard news of a new king

So they followed with gifts they thought to bring

Together they gathered to rejoice and to praise

Their hearts filled with wonder, love and amaze

And so on that night a great story began to unfold

A story of love which never gets old

It's there that the miracle of Christmas began

The birth of Jesus, the Saviour of Man!

Luke 2:1-7

Palm Sunday Glory

He rode on a donkey as the scriptures did say,

A new King of Peace

Was well on his way

They met him in hundreds

Lay palms in his stride,

A symbol of peace, the Prince of all Tides

Together they gathered

For a glimpse of the Lord

A king like no other, a king with no sword

"Blessed is the King who comes in the name of the Lord!"

they cheered and they cried,

A new dawn upon them

Their shepherd arrived!

Matthew 21:1-11

That Day

I had a dream I was there that day
When they came and took my Lord away
I watched when they lashed his back
And beat him on the dusty track
He carried his cross for you and for me
A sacrificial lamb for all to see
Not a word was uttered not even a sigh
For he knew the will of his Father up high
They took a crown and made it of thorn
Placed it on his head to laugh and to scorn
Then they took a nail and drove it in his hands
Fulfilling the scriptures, the king of all lands

I looked through the crowd and his mother I saw
Grief in her heart still standing tall
I wanted to cry out but no words could be found
By now my Lord hung on a cross wedged into the ground
He bowed his head, and took his last breath
The heavens cried out at the news of his death
They took a spear and pierced his side
A final blow, then end of the tide
Then the wind roared and the ground shook
Regret as they realised it was the Lord they took!

John 19:1-37

Risen !

Three days had passed since he lay in the tomb

Wrapped in cloth and covered by the moon,

The dawn of the Sabbath had brought a new day

And Mary of Magdala was well on her way

She brought with her spices and oils to infuse

But upon her arrival things seemed to confuse,

The great stone had moved and the entry unbound

Her Lord was taken and was nowhere to be found,

Then she heard a great voice and it danced in her heart

It took but a minute to tell them apart

His face was aglow like the light of the sun

His glory triumphant, the chosen One

It was her Lord Jesus, returned from the dead

Rejoice! He Has Risen, just as was said!

John 20:1-18

Holy Communion Gift

Come to me little child of mine
Your First Communion Day is here
Listen as I call your name
And hold your spirit near

Come to me little groom of Christ
And I'll meet you in my home
With this cup I share with you
Your sins I will atone

Come to me little bride of Christ
And you'll hunger no more
The bread of life you eat today
Holds the key to heaven's door

Child of God

I am a child of God
Taken to my heavenly home
To live beyond the clouds
Where the angels and saints roam

My Lord's prepared a place
For me to wait for you
To join me in his kingdom
When your earthly days are through

So do not shed your tears
Nor dwell in such despair
For the one who took me home
Has all the answers there

And when the day shall come
That the Lord shall call you home
I'll be there to meet you
Before His Holy Throne

Love without Christ

Love without Christ is not love at all

It is not fire, water

Thirst nor hunger

It is nor passion, touch

Life nor death

Love without Christ

Is like the wiltering flower in the drought

Which hopelessly awaits the rain

For only with Christ we can be born of water

And cleansed by fire

Only He can satisfy our yearning hunger with the bread
of life

And quench our thirst with His precious blood

It is Him we search in the face of another

And His love which conquers all, and brings forth life
from death

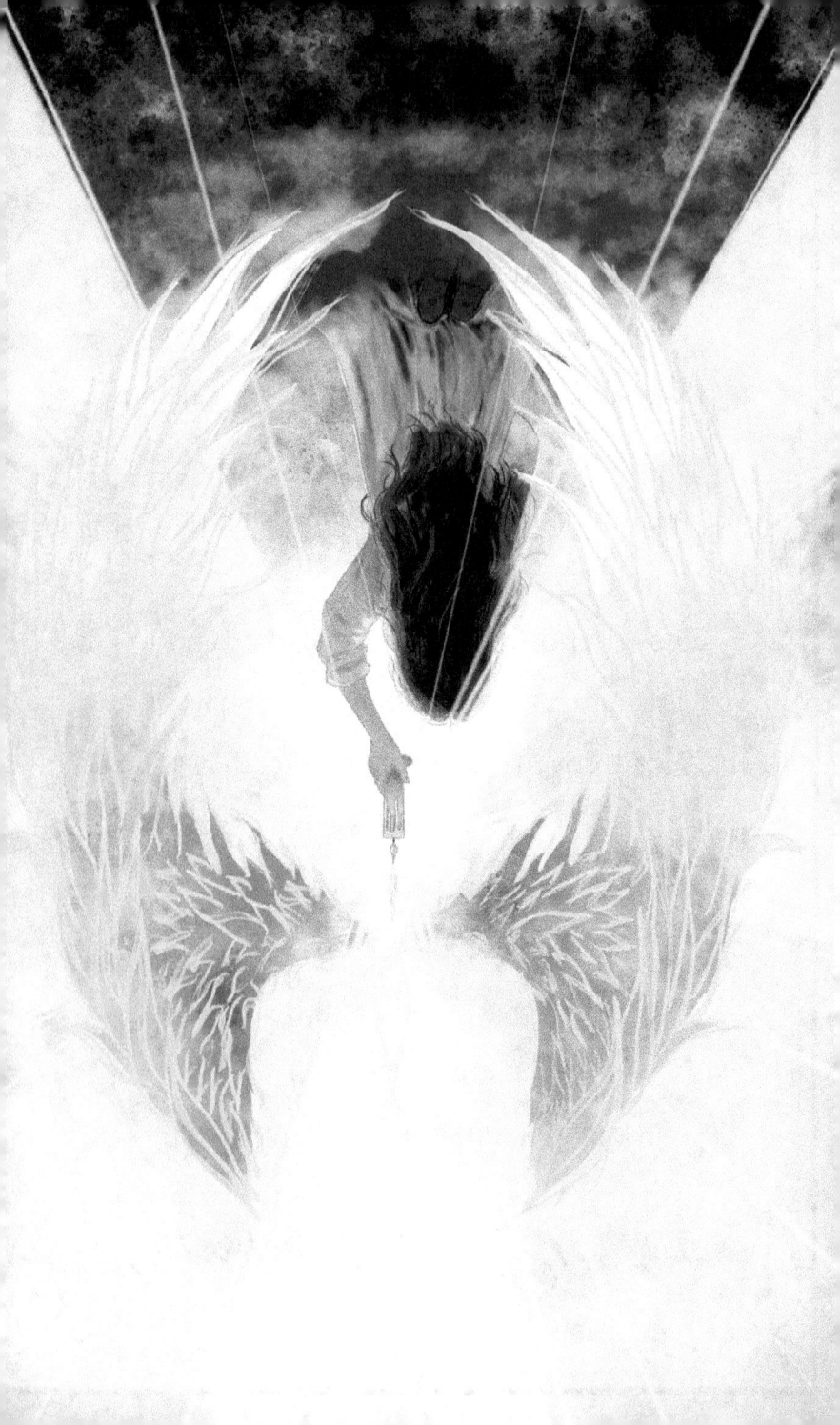

Angel of Mine

Guardian angel of mine
I ask you to shine
To watch over my spirit
And my loved ones in mind
Protector of God, you stand by his throne
My friend, my helper, you never leave me alone

Oh glorious angel, I lean on you still
I trust in you and the almighty's will
Though dangers seem near
Your pledge shows no fear
Be my shadow, I pray
Through night and through day
A promise to guide me
Out of all harm's way

I don't know your name
Only imagine your face
A beauty of God, pieced together with grace
I hear a soft voice and it tells me to hush
A comforting call, all dangers you crush
With wings of love and pure as a dove
A gift like no other sent from my Lord above

Jesus my Friend

My Lord and my God
How long must I remain captive to my own mind?
The corridors to my soul are a whirlwind of fears and torments
My heart is a lonely place
Mute must I be?
I dare not speak my Lord
For my words could destroy this world
But my heart speaks to you
And you understand my language
For everything that seems bitter is sweet
And all that appears sweet is bitter
And so I beg of you,
Jesus,
Will you be my friend?

On the pier I cried out to you

You have seen and heard my tears

It was not in vain

For your name is forever

And you remind me that my torments are little

A privilege

And yet I still have much to endure

"Hold fast," you whisper

For in the end your love will bring a glory that has no match for anything from this world

And Yes,

You are undoubtedly,

Forever, my Friend

Psalms 22:1-5

Part 3

Saint Michael

I dreamt I saw a man
Kneeling at God's gate
Hair ablaze and dressed
In a silver armoured plate
Behind him formed an army of white and
silver cloud
A gathering of angels
Standing tall and proud
Below him whirled a wind
Of fierce and angry smoke
Wails of anguish
And profanities they spoke
Above him flapped a flag
Embroidered white and red
Together with his wings
Pressed angelically overhead
He crossed himself and bowed before the
Kingdom of the Lord
And took an oath of honour
Upon his holy iron sword

Saint Anthony

I used to ask for help
When things had gone astray
Things I'd lost and forgotten
Along my travelled way
I'd call on Saint Anthony
To find and rediscover
But what I was really searching for
Was hiding under cover
It's a different prayer I send to the Doctor of the Church
A rediscovering of myself
An introspective search
Now I pray to find things that can't be seen or measured
Matters of the heart
Always to be treasured
I pray he helps me find my conscience
To live like saints do

To find my strength and use it

The way God wants me to

I pray he helps me find my courage

In the grief which plagues my mind

To continue on this course

No matter what struggles I may find

I pray he helps me find the right road to Jesus and

his throne

So I may one day join Christ

In his eternal heavenly home

Saint Rita

Thorn of Christ, born to love
Guider of the impossible from the heavens above
A mother, a wife and a widow too
Saint Rita of Cascia was one of few
She suffered much pain and abuse in her home
Many prayers were sent to the heavenly throne
Conversions were made
There was some peace
But sadly her home once again found the beast
She did not falter and prayed to the Lord
And angels were sent with a righteous sword
Christ saw her faith and he knew her heart
He wanted to give her his suffering in part
So he sent her a wound of agony and thorn
And from these sufferings a saint was born

Saint Padre Pio

Padre Pio the mystical friar
Your piety and faith was one to admire
Chosen to share in the signs of the Lord
Your wounds were a part of a heavenly reward
The devil would torment you alone at night
Even as a child he'd give you a fright
But you would not falter
And took your vows to live by the altar
Rosary in hand and head bowed in prayer
The love of the Lord was your only care
Confessions were heard from morning to night
How many wrongs you tried to make right
You promised to help us reach our heavenly goal
Loving Pio, help me and pray for my soul

Saint Joseph

I heard an echo across a deserted creek
So I followed along the track to have a little peak
I looked around and no one was to be found
Just a white flowering lily sprouting from the ground
Three white flowers stood tall amongst the grass
Free from the tramples of the travellers who had passed
I froze in time to think who could have planted such a
wonder?
Whose voice it was I'd heard, calling me under
It was then that I saw Saint Joseph appear
His purity and gentleness had been drawing me near
So before me stood the earthly father of my Lord
The one whose help I'd often implore
It was then that he placed the lily in my hand
And helped me to walk back home along the sand
It's there that he blessed me and vowed to be near
His call of love to be a weapon in my fear
And the lily, was clasped gently in my palm,
A reminder of the Trinity, magnificent and calm

Saint Francis of Assisi

If I could go back in time
There's a saint I'd make a friend of mine
We'd write together and sing along
And listen to the call of God to correct every wrong
He'd teach me how to live and forget
To leave all materials behind without regret
He'd show me how to live like Christ each day
And throw all my possessions away
To be pure of heart and nurture the poor
While we spread the Word of God some more
He'd lead me to the sick and the weak
To follow the virtues, be humble and meek
I'd dress like him in a brown hooded cloak
The Holy Spirit in crowds I'd watch him invoke
And best of all I'd witness the love between Saint Francis and my Lord
Unbreakable, like the Franciscan cord

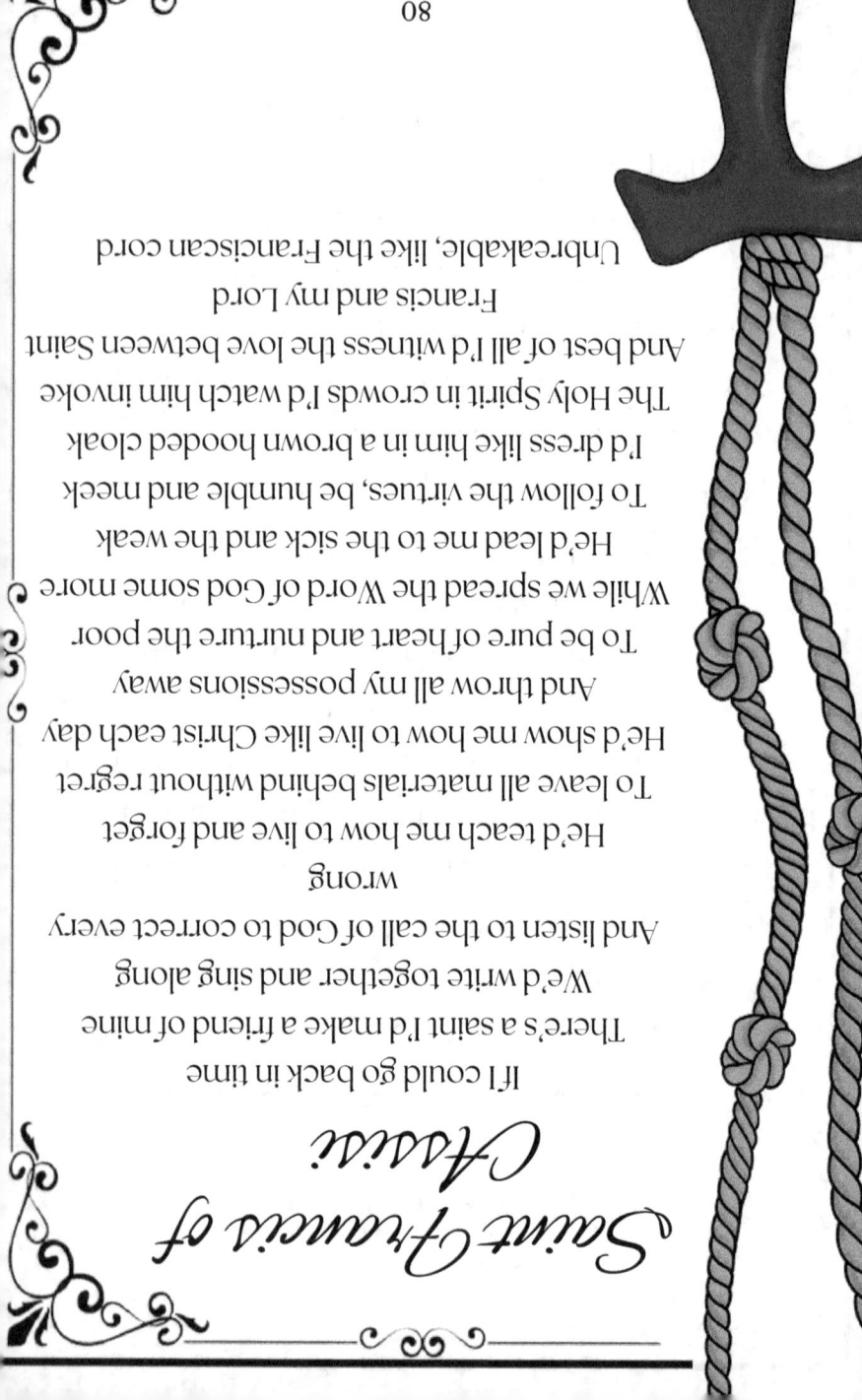

Saint Maximilian Kolbe

16670

The shadows of Auschwitz hold a glimmer of light
A memory of a friar who still shines bright
Dressed in blue stripes with a cross on his chest
He became a prisoner with a holy quest
A catholic, a priest but still a man
The numbers 16670 were tattooed to his hand
His pathway to Heaven began with a dream
A vision of Mary with a choice it seemed
Purity and martyrdom would be his call
And without hesitation he said "Yes" to all
Saint Maximilian Kolbe consecrated his heart
He and the Holy Mother were never apart
He lay down his life that another might live
To help those who suffered to love and forgive
And when his last hour was near
He showed those around him he felt no fear
For he knew what was waiting and his reward would be great
A greeting from Jesus at Heaven's gate

Saint Bernadette

There's a young saint who's special to me
A saint I prayed my child to be
It's her I've prayed to in the quiet of the night
Her intercession I implored, to make all things right
It was her blessed eyes so fresh and sweet
That saw Our Lady with roses at her feet
Her ears that heard our Mother's call
With a message of penance, necessary for all
Her lips which first tasted the holy springs
Thousands of miracles that water brings
Saint Bernadette of Lourdes holds my heart
I trust her and sweet Jesus are never apart
For this humble saint to whom the Virgin appeared in a grotto
Chose to love Christ as her unfaltering motto

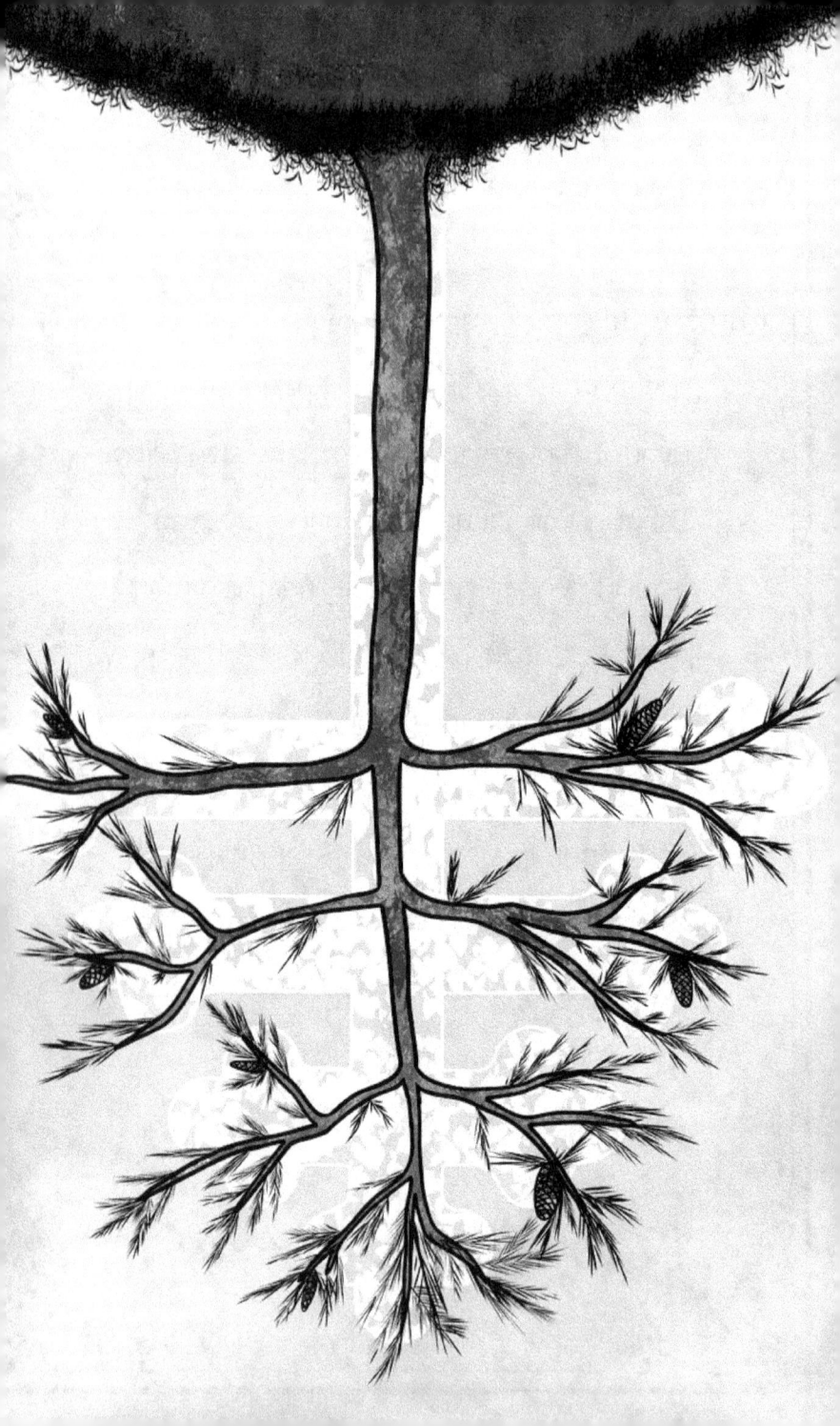

Saint Charbel

Deep in the Cedars where the clouds brush the mountains
Knelt a hooded monk with a love for God and his nations
His head bowed in prayer, it was his heart that spoke
Since silence became him from the moment he woke,
His home was simple, his pillow a stone
Each hour was spent adoring the Lord on his throne
His humility was rare and his piety a gift
He became the anchor in a nation adrift
Hermit of Lebanon and teacher for all

He would become the grandest of Cedar trees
Strong and tall
Its roots can be felt all over his land
But you needn't go there to feel his blessed hand
Countless miracles have been traced to his heart
Proof he has stood at God's altar and played his part
This blessed Saint who makes all things well
Once was a man who chose God and the name
Charbel